NATIONAL
GEOGRAPHIC
KiDS

Funny FILL-IN
MY ANCIENT EGYPT ADVENTURE

NATIONAL GEOGRAPHIC
WASHINGTON, D.C.

How to Play Funny Fill-In!

Love to create amazing stories? Good, because this one stars YOU. Get ready to laugh with all your friends—you can play with as many people as you want! Make sure to keep this book on your shelf. You'll want to read it again and again!

Are You Ready to Laugh?

- One person picks a story—you can start at the beginning, the middle, or the end of the book.

- Ask a friend to call out a word that the space asks for—noun, verb, or something else—and write it in the blank space. If there's more than one player, ask the next person to say a word. Extra points for creativity!

- When all the spaces are filled in, you have your very own Funny Fill-In. Read it out loud for a laugh.

- Want to play by yourself? Just fold over the page and use the cardboard insert at the back as a writing pad. Fill in the blank parts of speech list, and copy your answers into the story.

Fun Fact! Make sure you check out the amazing **Fun Facts** that appear on every page!

To play the game, you'll need to know how to form sentences. This list with examples of the parts of speech and other terms will help you get started:

Noun: The name of a person, place, thing, or idea
Examples: tree, mouth, creature
*The **ocean** is full of colorful **fish**.*

Adjective: A word that describes a noun or pronoun
Examples: green, lazy, friendly
*My **silly** dog won't stop laughing!*

Verb: An action word. In the present tense, a verb often ends in –s or –ing. If the space asks for past tense, changing the vowel or adding a –d or –ed to the end usually will set the sentence in the past.
Examples: swim, hide, plays, running (present tense); biked, rode, jumped (past tense)
*The giraffe **skips** across the savanna.*
*The flower **opened** after the rain.*

Adverb: A word that describes a verb and usually ends in –ly
Examples: quickly, lazily, soundlessly
*Kelley **greedily** ate all the carrots.*

Plural: More than one
Examples: mice, telephones, wrenches
*Why are all the **doors** closing?*

Silly Word or Exclamation: A funny sound, a made-up word, a word you think is totally weird, or a noise someone or something might make
Examples: Ouch! No way! Foozleduzzle! Yikes!
*"**Darn!**" shouted Jim. "These cupcakes are sour!"*

Specific Words: There are many more ways to make your story hilarious. When asked for something like a number, animal, or body part, write in something you think is especially funny.

- time
- something soft, plural
- electronic gadget
- adjective
- loud noise
- verb
- noun, plural
- adjective
- something in your bedroom
- adverb ending in –ly
- number
- animal
- noun, plural
- adverb ending in –ly
- snack food
- silly word
- verb ending in –s
- adjective
- body part

Fun Fact! LIKE MANY ANCIENT EGYPTIAN GODS, ISIS WAS MARRIED TO A RELATIVE— HER OWN BROTHER!

A Visit From a Goddess

It's _____ and I'm lying in _____ reading a book about ancient Egypt by the light of my
time _____ something soft, plural

_____ . The weather outside is _____ , and each time I hear a(n) _____ ,
electronic gadget _____ adjective _____ loud noise

I _____ and pull my _____ closer to me. A flash of lightning brightens the room
verb _____ noun, plural

for a split second. Then I hear the sound of _____ breathing—it's coming from my
adjective

_____ . _____ , I peer out into the darkness and see a(n) _____ -foot-
something in your bedroom _____ adverb ending in –ly _____ number

tall woman wearing a headdress of _____ feathers and _____ —it's the
animal _____ noun, plural

goddess Isis, who I was just reading about! _____ , I scream out, "_____ !"
adverb ending in –ly _____ snack food

"_____ ," she says, and _____ toward me. She hands me a(n) _____ tablet
silly word _____ verb ending in –s _____ adjective

etched with pictures. The instant my _____ touches it, there's another flash of light. But this
body part

time, when my eyes adjust, I realize I'm staring up at the sun.

verb

adjective

room in a house

body part, plural

pet, plural

a profession, plural

verb

adjective

something that floats

your favorite color

number

noun

adjective

verb

clothing item, plural

ancient year

Sailing the Nile

The sun above is scorching; it feels like I'm in a desert. Then I _____ around and realize: I *am* in a
                                                              verb

desert! This is totally _____—I was just in my _____ ! In my _____ I
                         adjective   room in a house   body part, plural

hold the tablet that the goddess gave me. Carved into it are pictures of _____ and _____ ,
                                                                          pet, plural   a profession, plural

among other things. I suddenly realize these are in hieroglyphics, the picture-based writing system of ancient

Egypt! Hoping to find help, I _____ to a nearby river. On its banks, I notice how _____
                              verb   adjective

it is—this must be the Nile! The captain of a(n) _____ sails past and offers me a ride, and I'm
                                                  something that floats

grateful for the ride when I see what's swimming around—_____ crocodiles! They flash
                                                          your favorite color

their _____-inch-long teeth and eye everyone on board. I cling tightly to my _____ and
       number   noun

show my _____ hieroglyphics to the other travelers. But they can't _____ it. I notice
         adjective   verb

their _____ look outdated and ask what year it is. "_____ ," they answer.
       clothing item, plural   ancient year

verb ending in –ing

verb ending in –ing

body part

adjective

large number

something huge, plural

your age

construction equipment

kitchen utensil, plural

liquid

number

favorite food

favorite beverage

favorite singer

electronic gadget

feeling

verb

noun

body part, plural

Fun Fact! THE GREAT PYRAMID WAS ONCE COVERED IN WHITE LIMESTONE AND TOPPED WITH GOLD

Hauling Rocks

I'm relieved when we finally reach land—all the _____ (verb ending in –ing) and _____ (verb ending in –ing) on the water has upset my _____ (body part). But as soon as we're ashore, I'm put to work—_____ (adjective) work. I'm placed in a pit with _____ (large number) other people. Our task: to dig up _____ (something huge, plural). Each one weighs about _____ (your age) tons. I wish we could use a(n) _____ (construction equipment), but it hasn't been invented yet. So instead we use _____ (kitchen utensil, plural) to dig. After a few hours of work, I wipe the _____ (liquid) from my brow. It's _____ (number) degrees, and I'm hungry and thirsty. Suddenly I remember they don't have _____ (favorite food) or _____ (favorite beverage) here. And no _____ (favorite singer)—or even a(n) _____ (electronic gadget) to listen to! I start to feel _____ (feeling) about this journey I've been sent on and decide to rest. I crawl up out of the pit, _____ (verb) behind a(n) _____ (noun), and close my _____ (body part, plural).

- animal
  - body part
- large number
  - noun, plural
- verb ending in –ing
  - exclamation
- verb
  - animal
- number
  - something gross
- liquid
  - silly word
- noun
  - same noun
- time
  - something hot
- adjective
  - insect, plural

Fun Fact!

TODAY MANY **ARCHAEOLOGISTS** USE **SATELLITES** TO FIND NEW TOMBS AND PYRAMIDS.

PHARAOH & ASSOC. CONSTRUCTION

COMING SPRING

Building Pyramids

I'm woken up by a(n) _____ licking my _____. On its back are _____ pounds
(animal) (body part) (large number)

of _____ for building pyramids. It's time to haul them to a site and start _____.
(noun, plural) (verb ending in –ing)

_____! I think. But then I cheer up: Maybe someone at the site can help me _____ my
(exclamation) (verb)

mystery hieroglyphics. I'm desperate to know what they say. I saddle up atop a(n) _____ and travel
(animal)

for _____ days and nights across the sand. At last, I see a construction site in the distance. We're greeted
(number)

with a meal of _____ and endless mugs of _____. It's all to give us energy for
(something gross) (liquid)

the job ahead: building pyramids for Pharaoh _____, _____ by _____.
(silly word) (noun) (same noun)

At _____, we report for duty, and I sign up to toil inside a half-built pyramid to escape the hot
(time)

_____. But because I can't read the _____ signs, I wind up in a finished
(something hot) (adjective)

pyramid, and it's crawling _____. Eek!
(insect, plural)

number

animal

body part

verb

adjective

something shiny, plural

verb ending in –ing

pet, plural

verb

something sticky

color

type of pattern

noun, plural

verb

adverb ending in –ly

noun

something round

verb

adjective

Fun Fact! KING TUT'S TOMB CONTAINED OVER 5,000 ARTIFACTS SUCH AS CHARIOTS AND JEWELS.

Trapped in a Tomb

Only _____ second(s) into working in the pyramid, a tiny _____ bites me on my _____ .
             number   animal   body part

Spooked, I _____ down a hallway and into a(n) _____ room. It's filled with
                verb   adjective

_____ and its walls are painted with pictures of people _____ . On their
something shiny, plural   verb ending in –ing

heads stand _____ . *Strange*, I think. I spot a small tunnel and _____ into it. For a
                 pet, plural   verb

while I push my way through _____ . Then I emerge into a chamber painted in _____
                              something sticky   color

_____ . Within its walls are life-size _____ . I stand inside one and then _____
type of pattern   noun, plural   verb

with recognition: It's for a mummy. _____ , I jump out and decide to head back. But just then a
                                      adverb ending in –ly

strong _____ shakes the building and knocks loose a(n) _____ , blocking my exit.
          noun   something round

With all my might, I try to move it. But it won't _____ . Then things get _____ :
                                                    verb   adjective

I remember I left my hieroglyphics in the other room.

- verb
- adjective
- verb ending in –ing
- verb ending in –ing
- noun
- something gross, plural
- verb
- something sharp, plural
- something tiny, plural
- body part, plural
- noun
- body part
- verb ending in –s
- famous city
- noun

Sandstorm!

I try not to _____ . I'm trapped in a room made for mummies—no _____ deal, right?
                    verb   adjective

Wrong. My heart is _____ and my palms are _____ —I've got to get out
                        verb ending in –ing   verb ending in –ing

of here! I spy a ray of light poking through a(n) _____ in the ceiling and start to climb the wall,
                                                            noun

dodging _____ on its surface. At the top, I _____ out of the tomb—and into
            something gross, plural   verb

a raging sandstorm. It feels like millions of little _____ are pricking my skin, and soon
                                                            something sharp, plural

_____ start to fill my mouth, ears, and nose. My _____ slightly open, I take off
something tiny, plural   body part, plural

running in search of shelter. I can only find a(n) _____ , though, so I place it on my _____
                                                        noun   body part

for protection. Soon the wind _____ it away and I'm totally exposed again. I stagger toward
                                    verb ending in –s

_____ , hoping to reach it before the _____ swallows me up.
famous city   noun

color

   color

adjective

   something dry, plural

noun, plural

   exclamation

verb

   body part, plural

adverb ending in –ly

   noun, plural

number

   sea creature, plural

cartoon character

   type of dinosaur

type of vegetable

   adjective

liquid

   something gross

verb

Fun Fact! ANCIENT EGYPTIANS SHAVED THEIR HEADS TO STAY COOL ... AND TO AVOID LICE!

THE OASIS

SAND-WICHES!

CAMEL-MILE TEA!

Lost in the Desert

Luckily, the storm stops. I'm _____ and _____ all over from the sand, though.
                                     color   *color*

My mouth is completely _____—the inside feels like _____. I look around
                                     adjective   *something dry, plural*

and see nothing but a sea of _____ surrounding me. _____! I think. I'm
                                     noun, plural   *exclamation*

lost in the desert. But then I _____ my _____ and see something shimmering in
                                    verb   *body part, plural*

the distance—an oasis! _____, I crawl over to it. But I stop dead in my _____
                         adverb ending in –ly   *noun, plural*

when I see what's there: _____ _____, _____, and a(n) _____.
                         number   *sea creature, plural*   *cartoon character*   *type of dinosaur*

They're all clustered around a giant _____. How _____. I ask where the _____
                                 type of vegetable   *adjective*   *liquid*

is and find out there is none—there's only _____ to quench my thirst. I have no choice but to
                                      something gross

pick it up, pucker up, and _____. Ew!
                              verb

Fun Fact! A CAMEL CAN DRINK UP TO 32 GALLONS (121 L) OF WATER AT ONE TIME.

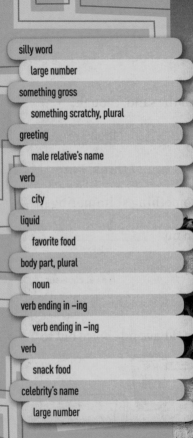

- silly word
- large number
- something gross
- something scratchy, plural
- greeting
- male relative's name
- verb
- city
- liquid
- favorite food
- body part, plural
- noun
- verb ending in –ing
- verb ending in –ing
- verb
- snack food
- celebrity's name
- large number

Herding Camels

"_____ , why are you drinking sand?!" I hear. I spin around and see a shepherd leading a herd
silly word

of _____ camels. They're very unpleasant, spitting _____ and chewing
large number   something gross

_____ . "_____ , I am _____ ," he says. I explain that I'm lost,
something scratchy, plural   greeting   male relative's name

and he makes me an offer: I help him _____ the camels back to _____ in exchange
verb   city

for _____ and _____ . We shake _____ and seal the deal. He hands
liquid   favorite food   body part, plural

me the _____ and I take over the herd. Within seconds, though, the camels are _____
noun   verb ending in –ing

and _____ , and I wonder whether I can keep control. Suddenly one breaks free and begins
verb ending in –ing

to _____ away from the herd. "_____ !" I shout, "I'm _____ !" This
verb   snack food   celebrity's name

seems to keep them in line, so I shout it over and over— _____ times, to be exact, by the
large number

time we reach the city.

19

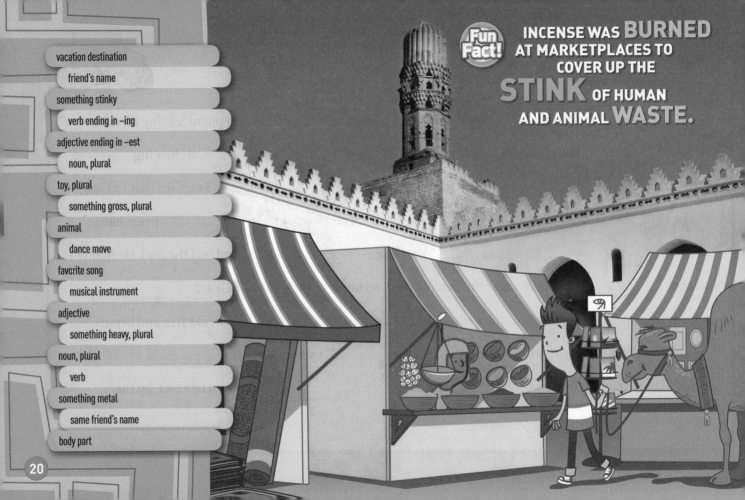

vacation destination

friend's name

something stinky

verb ending in –ing

adjective ending in –est

noun, plural

toy, plural

something gross, plural

animal

dance move

favorite song

musical instrument

adjective

something heavy, plural

noun, plural

verb

something metal

same friend's name

body part

Fun Fact! INCENSE WAS **BURNED** AT MARKETPLACES TO **COVER UP THE** **STINK** OF HUMAN AND ANIMAL **WASTE.**

At the city gates, the shepherd informs me he's leaving for _____ (vacation destination). He instructs me

to take his herd of camels to the marketplace and give them to his friend _____ (friend's name). I ask how to

find the market. "Follow the smell of _____ (something stinky)," he says, before _____ (verb ending in –ing) into the

crowd. I pick up the scent and sure enough it leads me to the _____ (adjective ending in –est) place I've ever been.

Shops selling _____ (noun, plural), giant _____ (toy, plural), and _____ (something gross, plural) stretch for miles.

A(n) _____ (animal) charmer is enticing his pet to _____ (dance move) by playing " _____ (favorite song) "

on a(n) _____ (musical instrument). A(n) _____ (adjective) woman is juggling _____ (something heavy, plural). Winding my

way through the narrow _____ (noun, plural), I grip the camels' reins. But still they _____ (verb) wildly

and knock over a(n) _____ (something metal). I apologize to the owner, who turns out to be _____ (same friend's name).

I introduce myself, then something catches my _____ (body part)—my hieroglyphics!

Fun Fact!

PHARAOHS OFTEN WORE A
CROWN FEATURING **WADJET,**
THE **COBRA-SHAPED** GODDESS
WHO PROTECTED KINGS.

- verb
- adjective
- a profession
- number
- something hard
- large number
- food
- body part, plural
- shape
- color
- color
- type of pattern
- your name
- verb
- adjective
- silly word
- adjective

22

A Crown for a Queen

I've found the marketplace metalsmith—who has my missing tablet of hieroglyphics! I hand over the camels

and _____ about the tablet. It turns out a(n) _____ _____ brought
         verb   *adjective*   *a profession*

it by, and the metalsmith will give it to me—if I work in the shop for _____ hours. I accept and
                                                                              number

get right to work helping construct a crown made of _____ . First I stoke the fire until it's a
                                                              something hard

scorching _____ degrees. Then I melt down the material until it's as soft as _____ .
              large number   *food*

Using my _____ , I sculpt it into a(n) _____ , then add beautiful _____ ,
              body part, plural   *shape*   *color*

_____ , and _____ gems. Across the top I inscribe the words "_____
  color   *type of pattern*   *your name*

was here." I let the crown _____ and then show it to the metalsmith. "I'm so _____ ,"
                                verb   *adjective*

the metalsmith cries, and asks me to present it to Pharaoh _____ and his wife, the Queen, at
                                                                  silly word

a(n) _____ feast that evening.
         adjective

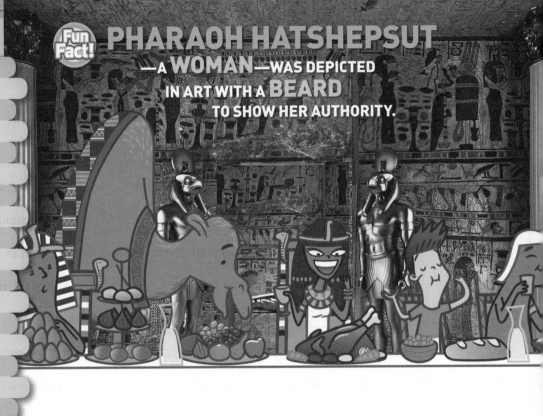

- adjective ending in –ed
- silly word
- friend's name
- celebrity's name
- color
- body part
- body part, plural
- noun
- verb
- verb ending in –s
- verb
- gymnastics move ending in –s
- your favorite song
- musical instrument
- adjective
- year
- verb
- foreign language

Fun Fact! PHARAOH HATSHEPSUT —A WOMAN—WAS DEPICTED IN ART WITH A BEARD TO SHOW HER AUTHORITY.

The Pharaoh, the Queen, and Me

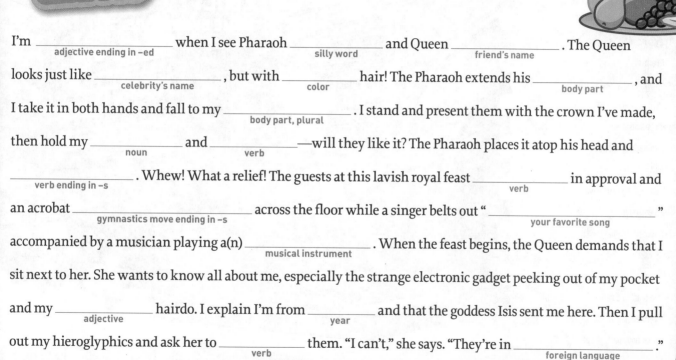

I'm _____ when I see Pharaoh _____ and Queen _____ . The Queen
　　　adjective ending in –ed　　　　　　　　　　silly word　　　　　　　　friend's name

looks just like _____ , but with _____ hair! The Pharaoh extends his _____ , and
　　　　　　celebrity's name　　　　　　color　　　　　　　　　　　　　body part

I take it in both hands and fall to my _____ . I stand and present them with the crown I've made,
　　　　　　　　　　　　　　　　body part, plural

then hold my _____ and _____—will they like it? The Pharaoh places it atop his head and
　　　　　　noun　　　　　　verb

_____ . Whew! What a relief! The guests at this lavish royal feast _____ in approval and
　verb ending in –s　　　　　　　　　　　　　　　　　　　　　　　　　　　　　verb

an acrobat _____ across the floor while a singer belts out " _____ "
　　　　gymnastics move ending in –s　　　　　　　　　　　　　　　　　　your favorite song

accompanied by a musician playing a(n) _____ . When the feast begins, the Queen demands that I
　　　　　　　　　　　　　　　musical instrument

sit next to her. She wants to know all about me, especially the strange electronic gadget peeking out of my pocket

and my _____ hairdo. I explain I'm from _____ and that the goddess Isis sent me here. Then I pull
　　　adjective　　　　　　　　　　　year

out my hieroglyphics and ask her to _____ them. "I can't," she says. "They're in _____ ."
　　　　　　　　　　　　　　verb　　　　　　　　　　　　　　　　　　　　foreign language

25

- exotic location
  - teacher's name
- body part, plural
  - verb
- number
  - type of food
- verb ending in –s
  - something enormous
- liquid
  - something expensive
- verb ending in –s
  - something shiny
- silly word
  - animal
- same teacher's name
  - verb ending in –s
- another body part, plural

The Pharaoh and the Queen are fascinated I'm from _____ . They want to add me to
exotic location

their royal staff, as the official caretaker of their cat, _____ . On my first day, I clip its
teacher's name

_____ and _____ between its toes, all _____ of them. Then I heat up a bowl
body part, plural   _verb_   _number_

of _____ , its dinner. Hungry, I try to sneak a bite, but the cat _____ at
type of food   _verb ending in –s_

me, and I back off. Next it's bathtime. I fill up a(n) _____ with warm _____ , then
something enormous   _liquid_

add a sprinkling of _____ —the Queen's special request. Turns out, though, the cat hates
something expensive

baths. It _____ and runs under a(n) _____ . I wiggle under and try to coax
verb ending in –s   _something shiny_

the cat out. "Here, _____ ," I say. No luck. Then I pull a(n) _____ out of my pocket
silly word   _animal_

and toss it under—that should work. It does: _____ _____ and leaps into
same teacher's name   _verb ending in –s_

my _____ . _Purr!_
another body part, plural

TUTANKHAMUN
WAS PROBABLY ONLY NINE YEARS OLD
WHEN HE BECAME PHARAOH.

- female friend's name
- male relative's name
- small number
- small number
- same friend's name
- verb
- toy, plural
- noun
- same relative's name
- something gross
- clothing item, plural
- command
- verb
- noun
- insect, plural
- verb
- electronic gadget
- verb
- noun

The Pharaoh thinks I did such a good job babysitting the cat that he puts me in charge of his children,

_____ and _____ . They're _____ and _____ —and
   female friend's name   male relative's name   small number   small number

royal pains, I soon find out. The first thing _____ does is demand that I _____ her
                                     same friend's name   verb

_____ . I have no choice—she's a(n) _____ , after all. So I get right to it. After a while I
   toy, plural   noun

notice that _____ has been awfully quiet. I look over and see he's smearing _____
              same relative's name   something gross

all over the Queen's _____ . "_____ !" I yell. He starts to _____ , then kicks
               clothing item, plural   command   verb

over a(n) _____ full of giant _____ that spill everywhere. Terrified, his sister starts to
    noun   insect, plural

_____ . Quickly, I pull out my _____ and show it to them. They're amazed. I promise
   verb   electronic gadget

they can _____ with it if they behave and clean up. They agree, and as they're throwing
    verb

the last _____ in the trash, the Pharaoh comes home.
   noun

adjective

    adverb ending in –ly

noun

    color

something sticky

    body part

animal

    noun, plural

favorite food

    liquid

another body part, plural

    noun, plural

something stinky

    verb

something shiny

    verb

favorite singer

Fun Fact! BOTH MEN AND WOMEN WORE KOHL, AN ANCIENT EYELINER MADE OF POISONOUS LEAD.

30

Beauty Secrets of the Ancients

It's day two of babysitting the royal pains. Today they want to "make me _____," the princess
_{adjective}

says. She'd like to show me her mother's beauty secrets. _____, I say yes. She commands me to
_{adverb ending in –ly}

sit in a(n) _____ then starts to rub what looks like _____ _____ all over
_{noun}   _{color}   _{something sticky}

my _____ . I ask what it is, and she tells me it's made from _____ poop. Yuck!
_{body part}   _{animal}

Strangely, though, it smells like _____ , so I don't mind too much. Next, she dabs a mixture of
_{noun, plural}

ground-up _____ and _____ around my _____ . "This will get rid
_{favorite food}   _{liquid}   _{another body part, plural}

of your _____ ," she tells me. She then reaches for a(n) _____—*Oh no*, I think. But
_{noun, plural}   _{something stinky}

just then my skin starts to _____ , so I call off the rest of the treatment. The princess holds up
_{verb}

a(n) _____ in front of me and I _____—I look just like _____ !
_{something shiny}   _{verb}   _{favorite singer}

Fun Fact!

KIDS IN ANCIENT EGYPT PLAYED A **HOCKEY-LIKE** **GAME** USING STICKS FROM **PALM BRANCHES.**

- number
- adjective
- liquid
- room in a house
- silly word
- verb
- noun
- color
- verb ending in –ing
- large number
- toy, plural
- clothing item
- adverb ending in –ly
- noun
- adverb ending in –ly
- something round
- command

32

It's day _____ of babysitting and the kids are starting to make me _____ . It's pouring
_____ number _____ _____ adjective

_____ outside, so we're holed up in the _____ for the afternoon. The
_____ liquid _____ _____ room in a house

prince pulls out a board game called _____ and asks the princess and me to _____ . We
_____ silly word _____ _____ verb

each pick a(n) _____—I choose the _____ one—and the game is on. An hour in, I
_____ noun _____ _____ color

realize the kids are _____—the prince has pocketed _____ coins from the board,
_____ verb ending in –ing _____ _____ large number

and the princess has stuffed a dozen _____ in her _____ . I _____
_____ toy, plural _____ _____ clothing item _____ adverb ending in –ly

end the game and threaten to take away their favorite _____ if I catch them cheating again.
_____ noun

_____ , the kids start kicking around a(n) _____ . Before I can
_____ adverb ending in –ly _____ _____ something round

say _____ , they send it smashing through a window. Through the hole,
_____ command

I can see the royal garden. I get an idea.

favorite place

a profession

verb

verb

verb ending in –ing

vegetable, plural

beverage

liquid

fruit, plural

food, plural

noun

animal, plural

food, plural

noun

verb ending in –ed

Fun Fact! FARM ANIMAL **DROPPINGS** WERE OFTEN USED TO TREAT **EYE INFECTIONS!**

I have a plan to get out of babysitting. I tell the Pharaoh that back in _____ , I was an expert
favorite place

_____ and I'd like to _____ in the royal garden instead. He agrees—it would be a
a profession   verb

shame to waste my talent. So I _____ the kids goodbye and report for duty. I quickly discover a
verb

problem with my plan: I'm clueless when it comes to _____ . I spray the _____
verb ending in –ing   vegetable, plural

with _____ instead of _____ . I accidentally mow the _____ . And I
beverage   liquid   fruit, plural

mistake the _____ for weeds and pull them out. But worst: I leave the _____ open,
food, plural   noun

and a herd of _____ wander in and eat all of the _____ then build a nest on
animal, plural   food, plural

the _____ . The head gardener demands I be _____ . But the Pharaoh takes mercy on me
noun   verb ending in –ed

and instead sends me to apprentice with an artist.

Fun Fact! OVER THE CENTURIES, TOMB ROBBERS HAVE STOLEN THE MAJORITY OF ANCIENT EGYPTIAN ART.

verb ending in –s

verb ending in –ing

noun

verb

adjective

animal

adjective

musical instrument

something squishy

verb

verb

verb ending in –s

type of plant

type of bird

something scary

adjective

exclamation

The royal artist takes one look at me and _____ . He knows I've been banned from
_____(verb ending in –s)_____

_____ in the _____ and that I was sent to _____ with him as a last
(verb ending in –ing)   (noun)   (verb)

resort. So we start with something _____ : drawing. I sketch a(n) _____ that I
                                      (adjective)   (animal)

think looks _____ . But when I show it to the artist, he compliments me instead on the beautiful
              (adjective)

_____ I've drawn. *Hmm*, I think. We switch to sculpting, and he hands me a lump of
(musical instrument)

_____ to mold into the Queen's likeness. I _____ and _____ , then present
(something squishy)   (verb)   (verb)

my work to the artist. He _____ and scolds me for sculpting _____ instead of the
                            (verb ending in –s)   (type of plant)

Queen. Next he asks me to simply paint a(n) _____ . But I can't even do that—my painting
                                              (type of bird)

looks more like a(n) _____ . He thinks of one last thing I might be _____ at: mummy-
                      (something scary)   (adjective)

making. _____ ! I think.
          (exclamation)

Fun Fact!

A **MUMMY'S** LIVER, STOMACH, INTESTINES, AND LUNGS WERE **REMOVED** AND **KEPT IN JARS.**

animal

mythical creature

male relative's name

large number

noun

body part

noun

famous athlete

adjective

clothing item

verb

dance move

verb

noun

noun

Making Mummies

Mummy-making requires the bravery of a(n) _____ (animal) and the patience of a(n) _____ (mythical creature). Or so I'm told by the master mummy-maker in ancient Egypt: _____ (male relative's name). Today he'll be teaching me how to make a mummy. To start, he hands me a(n) _____ (large number) -foot-long roll of linen. "We'll use this to wrap the mummy," he instructs. Next we move to a table where he'll show me how to use a(n) _____ (noun) to remove a mummy's _____ (body part) and place it in a(n) _____ (noun). Nearby lies a mummy that resembles _____ (famous athlete). I try not to look at it and focus on the teacher instead. Then suddenly I feel _____ (adjective) cold fingers grab my _____ (clothing item) —the mummy's alive! I _____ (verb) and we _____ (dance move) around the room, each of us trying to _____ (verb) the other. Luckily, the mummy takes a tumble and lands on a(n) _____ (noun) and I quickly throw a(n) _____ (noun) on top of it—Whew!

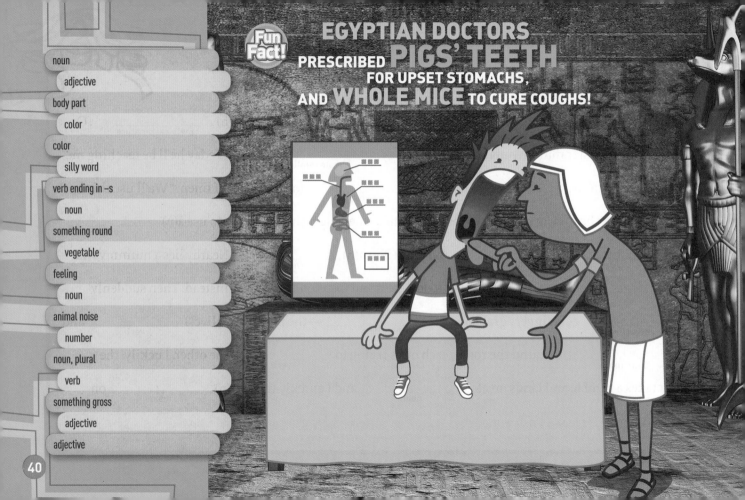

Ancient Remedies

I'm sitting on top of a trapped mummy, trying to catch my _____ . I just narrowly escaped

noun

after a(n) _____ chase. Once I calm down, I inspect myself and find I've hurt my

adjective

_____ . It's _____ and _____ and clearly needs medical attention. So

body part   color   color

my friend the Pharaoh gets me a visit with the royal physician. Dr. _____ _____

silly word   verb ending in –s

me right away. As he sets out his tools—a(n) _____ , _____ , and _____

noun   something round   vegetable

—I realize they do things a little differently here in ancient Egypt. I start to feel _____ . He tells

feeling

me to open wide, shoves a(n) _____ in my mouth, then asks me to say _____

noun   animal noise

_____ time(s). I do, and he scribbles some _____ in my chart. Then he asks me

number   noun, plural

to _____ a(n) _____ . It's _____ , but I do it anyway. Much to my

verb   something gross   adjective

surprise, when I'm finished I feel _____ —it worked!

adjective

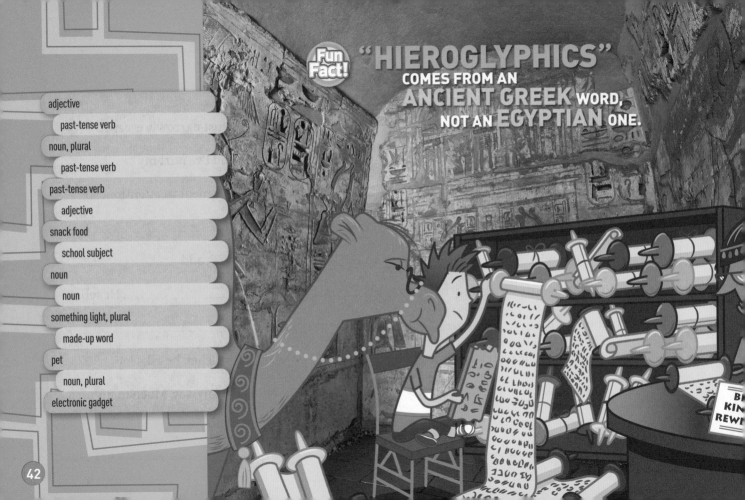

adjective

past-tense verb

noun, plural

past-tense verb

past-tense verb

adjective

snack food

school subject

noun

noun

something light, plural

made-up word

pet

noun, plural

electronic gadget

It's been pretty _____ since I _____ in ancient Egypt. I've explored
                         adjective   past-tense verb

_____ , _____ the royal family, and been _____ by a mummy.
   noun, plural   past-tense verb   past-tense verb

Now it's time to turn my attention to the reason I'm here: These _____ hieroglyphics given to me
                                                                        adjective

by the goddess Isis. I need to know more about her, so I head to the tomb of Pharaoh _____ to
                                                                                         snack food

visit the public library there. I remember reading about it in _____ class. Once there, I hand
                                                                  school subject

the hieroglyphics to the librarian and ask for her _____ . She pulls out an old _____ , blows
                                                       noun   noun

the _____ off of it, and starts to skim the pictures inside. "_____ ," she reads
    something light, plural   made-up word

aloud—then promptly turns into a(n) _____ . Thankfully, she can undo the spell and returns to
                                         pet

normal. She looks through the _____ again, then announces she's decoded my message. "These
                                 noun, plural

hieroglyphics are instructing you to reveal your _____ to the Egyptians," she says.
                                                   electronic gadget

Fun Fact!

AT **CEREMONIES** AND **FESTIVALS**, **MUSICIANS** PLAYED FLUTES, LUTES, TRUMPETS, HARPS, DRUMS, AND RATTLES.

- electronic gadget
- clothing item
- adjective
- time
- verb
- number
- reptile, plural
- number
- something sparkly, plural
- noun, plural
- silly word
- something enormous
- dance move
- year
- adverb ending in –ly
- same electronic gadget
- exclamation

From the Future

I pull my _____ out of my _____ and look at it. I can't believe this is why I've
          electronic gadget   *clothing item*

been sent back in time to ancient Egypt. What's more, I've been instructed to reveal it to the Egyptians during

a(n) _____ ceremony at _____ —today! The librarian who's helping me _____
        adjective   *time*   *verb*

the hieroglyphics reads me further instructions, and I write them down. I set off immediately, gathering

_____ _____ , _____ _____ , and a pair of _____ .
number   *reptile, plural*   *number*   *something sparkly, plural*   *noun, plural*

I ask Pharaoh _____ to gather everyone in a(n) _____ for my special
              silly word   *something enormous*

announcement. When the time comes, I _____ onstage and reveal that I'm from the year
                                      dance move

_____ and that the goddess Isis has sent me here to show them *this*. Very _____ , I pull
year   *adverb ending in –ly*

out my _____ . Everyone just stares. Then I remember to turn it on. "_____ !" the
       same electronic gadget   *exclamation*

crowd cries, and bows down.

noun

famous athlete

noun

verb

verb ending in –ing

noun

verb

adjective

noun

verb

shape

animal

time

amusement park

exotic animal, plural

famous historical figure

verb ending in –ing

noun

year in the past

Fun Fact! THE **PYRAMIDS** MAY HAVE BEEN BUILT AS **GIANT OBSERVATORIES** FOR **STUDYING** THE SKY.

After the unveiling of my _____ to the ancient Egyptians, I've become as famous as
                         noun

_____ . People shout my name and ask for my _____ , even at night when
  famous athlete   noun

I'm trying to _____ . So I decide it's time to head home. But how? After _____ with
              verb   verb ending in –ing

the Pharaoh, I visit an astronomer. He lays out a map and points to a(n) _____ . "There," he says.
                                                                          noun

"That's where we want to _____ ." I don't totally understand, but he seems _____ , so I
                         verb   adjective

follow his _____ . The next day, he has me _____ inside a(n) _____ painted
           noun   verb   shape

atop a(n) _____ . At precisely _____ there's a flash of light. I next expect to see the
          animal   time

familiar sites of home: _____ , _____ . But instead I see _____
                        amusement park   exotic animal, plural   famous historical figure

_____ in a(n) _____ ! There's been a mistake, I quickly realize. I've been accidentally
verb ending in –ing   noun

transported to the year _____ ! Time for another adventure.
                        year in the past

Credits

Published by the National Geographic Society

Gary E. Knell, *President and Chief Executive Officer*
John M. Fahey, *Chairman of the Board*
Declan Moore, *Executive Vice President; President, Publishing and Travel*
Melina Gerosa Bellows, *Publisher; Chief Creative Officer, Books, Kids, and Family*

Prepared by the Book Division

Hector Sierra, *Senior Vice President and General Manager*
Nancy Laties Feresten, *Senior Vice President, Kids Publishing and Media*
Jennifer Emmett, *Vice President, Editorial Director, Kids Books*
Eva Absher-Schantz, *Design Director, Kids Publishing and Media*
Jay Sumner, *Director of Photography, Kids Publishing*
R. Gary Colbert, *Production Director*
Jennifer A. Thornton, *Director of Managing Editorial*

Staff for This Book

Shelby Alinsky, *Project Editor*
James Hiscott, Jr., *Art Director*
Kelley Miller, *Senior Photo Editor*
Emily Krieger, *Writer*
Dan Sipple, *Illustrator*
Ariane Szu-Tu, *Editorial Assistant*
Callie Broaddus, *Design Production Assistant*
Margaret Leist, *Photo Assistant*
Grace Hill, *Associate Managing Editor*
Joan Gossett, *Production Editor*
Lewis R. Bassford, *Production Manager*
Susan Borke, *Legal and Business Affairs*

Production Services

Phillip L. Schlosser, *Senior Vice President*
Chris Brown, *Vice President, NG Book Manufacturing*
Rachel Faulise, *Manager*
Rahsaan Jackson, *Imaging*

Editorial, Design, and Production by Plan B Book Packagers

The National Geographic Society is one of the world's largest nonprofit scientific and educational organizations. Founded in 1888 to "increase and diffuse geographic knowledge," the Society's mission is to inspire people to care about the planet. It reaches more than 400 million people worldwide each month through its official journal, *National Geographic*, and other magazines; National Geographic Channel; television documentaries; music; radio; films; books; DVDs; maps; exhibitions; live events; school publishing programs; interactive media; and merchandise. National Geographic has funded more than 10,000 scientific research, conservation, and exploration projects and supports an education program promoting geographic literacy.

For more information, please call 1-800-NGS LINE (647-5463) or write to the following address:

National Geographic Society, 1145 17th Street N.W.
Washington, D.C. 20036-4688 U.S.A.

Visit us online at nationalgeographic.com/books

For librarians and teachers: ngchildrensbooks.org

More for kids from National Geographic: kids.nationalgeographic.com

For information about special discounts for bulk purchases, please contact National Geographic Books Special Sales: ngspecsales@ngs.org

For rights or permissions inquiries, please contact National Geographic Books Subsidiary Rights: ngbookrights@ngs.org

ISBN: 978-1-4263-1707-1

Printed in Hong Kong

14/THK/1